WALKING IN THE PROMISES OF GOD

Daily Meditation Scriptures

457 Bible Verses of God's Unfailing Promises

ISBN: 978-1-958404-69-0 (paperback)

Printed in United States of America

2 CORINTHIANS 1:19-20

For the Son of God, Jesus Christ, who was preached among you by us, *even* by me and Silvanus and Timothy, was not yea and nay, but in him is yea. For how many soever be the promises of God, in him is the yea: wherefore also through him is the Amen, unto the glory of God through us.

2 PETER 3:9

The Lord is not slack concerning his promise, as some count slackness; but is longsuffering to you-ward, not wishing that any should perish, but that all should come to repentance.

All of God's promises are "Yes" and "Amen" in Christ Jesus. What God has spoken, He is faithful to perform. There is no uncertainty in Him. The key, then, is to know what God has said.

The Word of God is our defense, our foundation, and our rule of faith. It is the standard by which we are to live. Yet many believers are trying to walk with God without truly knowing His Word. That posture leaves room for confusion, instability, and error.

As I reflect on my younger years, I remember how deeply Bible-centered many of our church activities were, especially in youth and children's ministry. One of the most meaningful practices was Scripture memorization. Our leaders found creative ways to help us hide the Word in our hearts, and much of what we learned has remained with us even now, decades later.

Today, many Christians can quote John 3:16, recite the Lord's Prayer, and remember portions of Psalms 23 and 100. Yet beyond these familiar passages, Scripture memorization is becoming less common. That is a great loss, because the Word of God was never meant to sit only on the page. It was meant to live in us.

Walking in the Promises of God was created to help restore that sacred practice. This book is not merely for reading, but for use. It is a tool to help individuals, families, churches, and groups return to the life-giving discipline of memorizing Scripture.

Use it during personal devotion. Use it in the home. Use it in small groups, Bible studies, youth meetings, and classrooms. Make it an activity. Make it a challenge. Make it a habit.

When the Word of God is deeply planted in the heart and firmly fixed in the memory, it will shape your thinking, strengthen your faith, guard your life, and transform your walk with God.

That is the purpose of this book.

And that is the power of His Word.

GENESIS 1:26-28

And God said, Let us make man in our image, after our likeness: and let them have dominion over the fish of the sea, and over the birds of the heavens, and over the cattle, and over all the earth, and over every creeping thing that creepeth upon the earth. And God created man in his own image, in the image of God created he him; male and female created he them. And God blessed them: and God said unto them, Be fruitful, and multiply, and replenish the earth, and subdue it; and have dominion over the fish of the sea, and over the birds of the heavens, and over every living thing that moveth upon the earth.

GENESIS 12:2-3

and I will make of thee a great nation, and I will bless thee, and make thy name great; and be thou a blessing: and I will bless them that bless thee, and him that curseth thee will I curse: and in thee shall all the families of the earth be blessed.

GENESIS 15:6

And he believed in Jehovah; and he reckoned it to him for righteousness.

GENESIS 17:2

And I will make my covenant between me and thee, and will multiply thee exceedingly.

GENESIS 18:14

Is anything too hard for Jehovah? At the set time I will return unto thee, when the season cometh round, and Sarah shall have a son.

GENESIS 18:19

For I have known him, to the end that he may command his children and his household after him, that they may keep the way of Jehovah, to do righteousness and justice; to the end that Jehovah may bring upon Abraham that which he hath spoken of him.

GENESIS 18:25

That be far from thee to do after this manner, to slay the righteous with the wicked, that so the righteous should be as the wicked; that be far from thee: shall not the Judge of all the earth do right?

GENESIS 22:17-18

that in blessing I will bless thee, and in multiplying I will multiply thy seed as the stars of the heavens, and as the sand which is upon the sea-shore; and thy seed shall possess the gate of his enemies; and in thy seed shall all the nations of the earth be blessed; because thou hast obeyed my voice.

EXODUS 6:7

and I will take you to me for a people, and I will be to you a God; and ye shall know that I am Jehovah your God, who bringeth you out from under the burdens of the Egyptians.

EXODUS 15:17

Thou wilt bring them in, and plant them in the mountain of thine inheritance, the place, O Jehovah, which thou hast made for thee to dwell in, The sanctuary, O Lord, which thy hands have established.

EXODUS 17:15

And Moses built an altar, and called the name of it Jehovah-nissi;

EXODUS 19:5-6

Now therefore, if ye will obey my voice indeed, and keep my covenant, then ye shall be mine own possession from among all peoples: for all the earth is mine: and ye shall be unto me a kingdom of priests, and a holy nation. These are the words which thou shalt speak unto the children of Israel.

EXODUS 33:14

And he said, My presence shall go *with thee*, and I will give thee rest.

EXODUS 34:6-7

And Jehovah passed by before him, and proclaimed, Jehovah, Jehovah, a God merciful and gracious, slow to anger, and abundant in lovingkindness and truth; keeping lovingkindness for thousands, forgiving iniquity and transgression and sin; and that will by no means clear *the guilty*, visiting the iniquity of the fathers upon the children, and upon the children's children, upon the third and upon the fourth generation.

LEVITICUS 10:3

Then Moses said unto Aaron, This is it that Jehovah spake, saying, I will be sanctified in them that come nigh me, and before all the people I will be glorified. And Aaron held his peace.

LEVITICUS 17:11

For the life of the flesh is in the blood; and I have given it to you upon the altar to make atonement for your souls: for it is the blood that maketh atonement by reason of the life.

LEVITICUS 18:5

Ye shall therefore keep my statutes, and mine ordinances; which if a man do, he shall live in them: I am Jehovah.

LEVITICUS 20:7-8

Sanctify yourselves therefore, and be ye holy; for I am Jehovah your God. And ye shall keep my statutes, and do them: I am Jehovah who sanctifieth you.

LEVITICUS 20:26

And ye shall be holy unto me: for I, Jehovah, am holy, and have set you apart from the peoples, that ye should be mine.

LEVITICUS 26:12-13

And I will walk among you, and will be your God, and ye shall be my people. I am Jehovah your God, who brought you forth out of the land of Egypt, that ye should not be their bondmen; and I have broken the bars of your yoke, and made you go upright.

NUMBERS 6:24-26

Jehovah bless thee, and keep thee: Jehovah make his face to shine upon thee, and be gracious unto thee: Jehovah lift up his countenance upon thee, and give thee peace.

NUMBERS 11:23

And Jehovah said unto Moses, Is Jehovah's hand waxed short? now shalt thou see whether my word shall come to pass unto thee or not.

NUMBERS 15:41

I am Jehovah your God, who brought you out of the land of Egypt, to be your God: I am Jehovah your God.

NUMBERS 23:19

God is not a man, that he should lie, neither the son of man, that he should repent: Hath he said, and will he not do it? Or hath he spoken, and will he not make it good?

DEUTERONOMY 1:10-11

Jehovah your God hath multiplied you, and, behold, ye are this day as the stars of heaven for multitude. Jehovah, the God of your fathers, make you a thousand times as many as ye are, and bless you, as he hath promised you!

DEUTERONOMY 1:30-31

Jehovah your God who goeth before you, he will fight for you, according to all that he did for you in Egypt before your eyes, and in the wilderness, where thou hast seen how that Jehovah thy God bare thee, as a man doth bear his son, in all the way that ye went, until ye came unto this place.

DEUTERONOMY 2:7

For Jehovah thy God hath blessed thee in all the work of thy hand; he hath known thy walking through this great wilderness: these forty years Jehovah thy God hath been with thee; thou hast lacked nothing.

DEUTERONOMY 3:22

Ye shall not fear them; for Jehovah your God, he it is that fighteth for you.

DEUTERONOMY 3:24

O Lord Jehovah, thou hast begun to show thy servant thy greatness, and thy strong hand: for what god is there in heaven or in earth, that can do according to thy works, and according to thy mighty acts?

DEUTERONOMY 4:7

For what great nation is there, that hath a god so nigh unto them, as Jehovah our God is whensoever we call upon him?

DEUTERONOMY 4:29

But from thence ye shall seek Jehovah thy God, and thou shalt find him, when thou searchest after him with all thy heart and with all thy soul.

DEUTERONOMY 4:31

for Jehovah thy God is a merciful God; he will not fail thee, neither destroy thee, nor forget the covenant of thy fathers which he sware unto them.

DEUTERONOMY 4:35, 39

Unto thee it was showed, that thou mightest know that Jehovah he is God; there is none else besides him. Know therefore this day, and lay it to thy heart, that Jehovah he is God in heaven above and upon the earth beneath; there is none else.

DEUTERONOMY 7:9

Know therefore that Jehovah thy God, he is God, the faithful God, who keepeth covenant and lovingkindness with them that love him and keep his commandments to a thousand generations.

DEUTERONOMY 18:17-18

And Jehovah said unto me, They have well said that which they have spoken. I will raise them up a prophet from among their brethren, like unto thee; and I will put my words in his mouth, and he shall speak unto them all that I shall command him.

DEUTERONOMY 20:4

for Jehovah your God is he that goeth with you, to fight for you against your enemies, to save you.

DEUTERONOMY 29:29

The secret things belong unto Jehovah our God; but the things that are revealed belong unto us and to our children for ever, that we may do all the words of this law.

JOSHUA 1:8

This book of the law shall not depart out of thy mouth, but thou shalt meditate thereon day and night, that thou mayest observe to do according to all that is written therein: for then thou shalt make thy way prosperous, and then thou shalt have good success.

JOSHUA 1:9

Have not I commanded thee? Be strong and of good courage; be not affrighted, neither be thou dismayed: for Jehovah thy God is with thee whithersoever thou goest.

JOSHUA 2:11

And as soon as we had heard it, our hearts did melt, neither did there remain any more spirit in any man, because of you: for Jehovah your God, he is God in heaven above, and on earth beneath.

JOSHUA 21:43-45

So Jehovah gave unto Israel all the land which he sware to give unto their fathers; and they possessed it, and dwelt therein. And Jehovah gave them rest round about, according to all that he sware unto their fathers: and there stood not a man of all their enemies before them; Jehovah delivered all their enemies into their hand. There failed not aught of any good thing which Jehovah had spoken unto the house of Israel; all came to pass.

JOSHUA 23:14

And, behold, this day I am going the way of all the earth: and ye know in all your hearts and in all your souls, that not one thing hath failed of all the good things which Jehovah your God spake concerning you; all are come to pass unto you, not one thing hath failed thereof.

RUTH 2:12

Jehovah recompense thy work, and a full reward be given thee of Jehovah, the God of Israel, under whose wings thou art come to take refuge.

RUTH 4:14

And the women said unto Naomi, Blessed be Jehovah, who hath not left thee this day without a near kinsman; and let his name be famous in Israel.

I SAMUEL 2:2

There is none holy as Jehovah; for there is none besides thee, neither is there any rock like our God.

I SAMUEL 2:6-8

Jehovah killeth, and maketh alive: He bringeth down to Sheol, and bringeth up. Jehovah maketh poor, and maketh rich: He bringeth low, he also lifteth up. He raiseth up the poor out of the dust, He lifteth up the needy from the dunghill, to make them sit with princes, and inherit the throne of glory: for the pillars of the earth are Jehovah's, and he hath set the world upon them.

I SAMUEL 2:9

He will keep the feet of his holy ones; but the wicked shall be put to silence in darkness; for by strength shall no man prevail.

I SAMUEL 2:30

Therefore Jehovah, the God of Israel, saith, I said indeed that thy house, and the house of thy father, should walk before me for ever: but now Jehovah saith, Be it far from me; for them that honor me I will honor, and they that despise me shall be lightly esteemed.

I SAMUEL 7:3

And Samuel spake unto all the house of Israel, saying, If ye do return unto Jehovah with all your heart, then put away the foreign gods and the Ashtaroth from among you, and direct your hearts unto Jehovah, and serve him only; and he will deliver you out of the hand of the Philistines.

I SAMUEL 10:19

but ye have this day rejected your God, who himself saveth you out of all your calamities and your distresses; and ye have said unto him, *Nay*, but set a king over us. Now therefore present yourselves before Jehovah by your tribes, and by your thousands.

I SAMUEL 12:21-22

and turn ye not aside; for *then would ye go* after vain things which cannot profit nor deliver, for they are vain. For Jehovah will not forsake his people for his great name's sake, because it hath pleased Jehovah to make you a people unto himself.

I SAMUEL 14:6

And Jonathan said to the young man that bare his armor, Come, and let us go over unto the garrison of these uncircumcised: it may be that Jehovah will work for us; for there is no restraint to Jehovah to save by many or by few.

I SAMUEL 15:29

And also the Strength of Israel will not lie nor repent; for he is not a man, that he should repent.

I SAMUEL 16:7

But Jehovah said unto Samuel, Look not on his countenance, or on the height of his stature; because I have rejected him: for *Jehovah seeth* not as man seeth; for man looketh on the outward appearance, but Jehovah looketh on the heart.

I SAMUEL 17:47

and that all this assembly may know that Jehovah saveth not with sword and spear: for the battle is Jehovah's, and he will give you into our hand.

I SAMUEL 26:23

And Jehovah will render to every man his righteousness and his faithfulness; forasmuch as Jehovah delivered thee into my hand to-day, and I would not put forth my hand against Jehovah's anointed.

2 SAMUEL 7:11-14

and *as* from the day that I commanded judges to be over my people Israel; and I will cause thee to rest from all thine enemies. Moreover Jehovah telleth thee that Jehovah will make thee a house. When thy days are fulfilled, and thou shalt sleep with thy fathers, I will set up thy seed after thee, that shall proceed out of thy bowels, and I will establish his kingdom. He shall build a house for my name, and I will establish the throne of his kingdom for ever. I will be his father, and he shall be my son: if he commit iniquity, I will chasten him with the rod of men, and with the stripes of the children of men;

2 SAMUEL 7:16

And thy house and thy kingdom shall be made sure for ever before thee: thy throne shall be established for ever.

2 SAMUEL 7:22

Wherefore thou art great, O Jehovah God: for there is none like thee, neither is there any God besides thee, according to all that we have heard with our ears.

2 SAMUEL 7:28

And now, O Lord Jehovah, thou art God, and thy words are truth, and thou hast promised this good thing unto thy servant:

2 SAMUEL 10:12

Be of good courage, and let us play the man for our people, and for the cities of our God: and Jehovah do that which seemeth him good.

2 SAMUEL 14:14

For we must needs die, and are as water spilt on the ground, which cannot be gathered up again; neither doth God take away life, but deviseth means, that he that is banished be not an outcast from him.

2 SAMUEL 22:4

I will call upon Jehovah, who is worthy to be praised: so shall I be saved from mine enemies.

2 SAMUEL 22:31-33

As for God, his way is perfect: the word of Jehovah is tried; He is a shield unto all them that take refuge in him. For who is God, save Jehovah? And who is a rock, save our God? God is my strong fortress; and he guideth the perfect in his way.

I KINGS 2:2-3

I am going the way of all the earth: be thou strong therefore, and show thyself a man; and keep the charge of Jehovah thy God, to walk in his ways, to keep his statutes, *and* his commandments, and his ordinances, and his testimonies, according to that which is written in the law of Moses, that thou mayest prosper in all that thou doest, and whithersoever thou turnest thyself.

I KINGS 8:23

and he said, O Jehovah, the God of Israel, there is no God like thee, in heaven above, or on earth beneath; who keepest covenant and lovingkindness with thy servants, that walk before thee with all their heart.

I KINGS 8:56-58

Blessed be Jehovah, that hath given rest unto his people Israel, according to all that he promised: there hath not failed one word of all his good promise, which he promised by Moses his servant. Jehovah our God be with us, as he was with our fathers: let him not leave us, nor forsake us; that he may incline our hearts unto him, to walk in all his ways, and to keep his commandments, and his statutes, and his ordinances, which he commanded our fathers.

2 KINGS 5:15

And he returned to the man of God, he and all his company, and came, and stood before him; and he said, Behold now, I know that there is no God in all the earth, but in Israel: now therefore, I pray thee, take a present of thy servant.

2 KINGS 6:16

And he answered, Fear not; for they that are with us are more than they that are with them.

2 KINGS 8:19

Howbeit Jehovah would not destroy Judah, for David his servant's sake, as he promised him to give unto him a lamp for his children alway.

2 KINGS 13:23

But Jehovah was gracious unto them, and had compassion on them, and had respect unto them, because of his covenant with Abraham, Isaac, and Jacob, and would not destroy them, neither cast he them from his presence as yet.

2 KINGS 17:39

but Jehovah your God shall ye fear; and he will deliver you out of the hand of all your enemies.

2 KINGS 19:25

Hast thou not heard how I have done it long ago, and formed it of ancient times? now have I brought it to pass, that it should be thine to lay waste fortified cities into ruinous heaps.

2 KINGS 19:30

And the remnant that is escaped of the house of Judah shall again take root downward, and bear fruit upward.

I CHRONICLES 4:10

And Jabez called on the God of Israel, saying, Oh that thou wouldest bless me indeed, and enlarge my border, and that thy hand might be with me, and that thou wouldest keep me from evil, that it be not to my sorrow! And God granted him that which he requested.

I CHRONICLES 16:10-12

Glory ye in his holy name; Let the heart of them rejoice that seek Jehovah. Seek ye Jehovah and his strength; Seek his face evermore. Remember his marvellous works that he hath done, His wonders, and the judgments of his mouth.

I CHRONICLES 16:25-27

For great is Jehovah, and greatly to be praised: He also is to be feared above all gods. For all the gods of the peoples are idols: but Jehovah made the heavens. Honor and majesty are before him: Strength and gladness are in his place.

I CHRONICLES 16:34

O give thanks unto Jehovah; for he is good; For his lovingkindness *endureth* for ever.

I CHRONICLES 17:10-14

and *as* from the day that I commanded judges to be over my people Israel; and I will subdue all thine enemies. Moreover I tell thee that Jehovah will build thee a house. And it shall come to pass, when thy days are fulfilled that thou must go to be with thy fathers, that I will set up thy seed after thee, who shall be of thy sons; and I will establish his kingdom. He shall build me a house, and I will establish his throne for ever. I will be his father, and he shall be my son: and I will not take my lovingkindness away from him, as I took it from him that was before thee; but I will settle him in my house and in my kingdom for ever; and his throne shall be established for ever.

I CHRONICLES 17:20-22

O Jehovah, there is none like thee, neither is there any God besides thee, according to all that we have heard with our ears. And what one nation in the earth is like thy people Israel, whom God went to redeem unto himself for a people, to make thee a name by great and terrible things, in driving out nations from before thy people, whom thou redeemedst out of Egypt? For thy people Israel didst thou make thine own people for ever; and thou, Jehovah, becamest their God.

I CHRONICLES 22:9-10

Behold, a son shall be born to thee, who shall be a man of rest; and I will give him rest from all his enemies round about; for his name shall be Solomon, and I will give peace and quietness unto Israel in his days. He shall build a house for my name; and he shall be my son, and I will be his father; and I will establish the throne of his kingdom over Israel for ever.

I CHRONICLES 28:9

And thou, Solomon my son, know thou the God of thy father, and serve him with a perfect heart and with a willing mind; for Jehovah searcheth all hearts, and understandeth all the imaginations of the thoughts. If thou seek him, he will be found of thee; but if thou forsake him, he will cast thee off for ever.

I CHRONICLES 29:14

But who am I, and what is my people, that we should be able to offer so willingly after this sort? for all things come of thee, and of thine own have we given thee.

2 CHRONICLES 6:14-15

and he said, O Jehovah, the God of Israel, there is no God like thee, in heaven, or on earth; who keepest covenant and lovingkindness with thy servants, that walk before thee with all their heart; who hast kept with thy servant David my father that which thou didst promise him: yea, thou spakest with thy mouth, and hast fulfilled it with thy hand, as it is this day.

2 CHRONICLES 7:14-16

if my people, who are called by my name, shall humble themselves, and pray, and seek my face, and turn from their wicked ways; then will I hear from heaven, and will forgive their sin, and will heal their land. Now mine eyes shall be open, and mine ears attent, unto the prayer that is made in this place. For now have I chosen and hallowed this house, that my name may be there for ever; and mine eyes and my heart shall be there perpetually.

2 CHRONICLES 14:11

And Asa cried unto Jehovah his God, and said, Jehovah, there is none besides thee to help, between the mighty and him that hath no strength: help us, O Jehovah our God; for we rely on thee, and in thy name are we come against this multitude. O Jehovah, thou art our God; let not man prevail against thee.

2 CHRONICLES 15:2

and he went out to meet Asa, and said unto him, Hear ye me, Asa, and all Judah and Benjamin: Jehovah is with you, while ye are with him; and if ye seek him, he will be found of you; but if ye forsake him, he will forsake you.

2 CHRONICLES 15:4

but when in their distress they turned unto Jehovah, the God of Israel, and sought him, he was found of them.

2 CHRONICLES 15:7

But be ye strong, and let not your hands be slack; for your work shall be rewarded.

2 CHRONICLES 16:9

For the eyes of Jehovah run to and fro throughout the whole earth, to show himself strong in the behalf of them whose heart is perfect toward him. Herein thou hast done foolishly; for from henceforth thou shalt have wars.

2 CHRONICLES 19:7

Now therefore let the fear of Jehovah be upon you; take heed and do it: for there is no iniquity with Jehovah our God, nor respect of persons, nor taking of bribes.

2 CHRONICLES 20:15

and he said, Hearken ye, all Judah, and ye inhabitants of Jerusalem, and thou king Jehoshaphat: Thus saith Jehovah unto you, Fear not ye, neither be dismayed by reason of this great multitude; for the battle is not yours, but God's.

2 CHRONICLES 20:20

And they rose early in the morning, and went forth into the wilderness of Tekoa: and as they went forth, Jehoshaphat stood and said, Hear me, O Judah, and ye inhabitants of Jerusalem: believe in Jehovah your God, so shall ye be established; believe his prophets, so shall ye prosper.

2 CHRONICLES 30:9

For if ye turn again unto Jehovah, your brethren and your children shall find compassion before them that led them captive, and shall come again into this land: for Jehovah your God is gracious and merciful, and will not turn away his face from you, if ye return unto him.

2 CHRONICLES 32:7-8

Be strong and of good courage, be not afraid nor dismayed for the king of Assyria, nor for all the multitude that is with him; for there is a greater with us than with him: with him is an arm of flesh; but with us is Jehovah our God to help us, and to fight our battles. And the people rested themselves upon the words of Hezekiah king of Judah.

EZRA 7:10

For Ezra had set his heart to seek the law of Jehovah, and to do it, and to teach in Israel statutes and ordinances.

EZRA 8:22

For I was ashamed to ask of the king a band of soldiers and horsemen to help us against the enemy in the way, because we had spoken unto the king, saying, The hand of our God is upon all them that seek him, for good; but his power and his wrath is against all them that forsake him.

EZRA 9:8-9

And now for a little moment grace hath been showed from Jehovah our God, to leave us a remnant to escape, and to give us a nail in his holy place, that our God may lighten our eyes, and give us a little reviving in our bondage. For we are bondmen; yet our God hath not forsaken us in our bondage, but hath extended lovingkindness unto us in the sight of the kings of Persia, to give us a reviving, to set up the house of our God, and to repair the ruins thereof, and to give us a wall in Judah and in Jerusalem.

NEHEMIAH 1:5-6

and said, I beseech thee, O Jehovah, the God of heaven, the great and terrible God, that keepeth covenant and lovingkindness with them that love him and keep his commandments: Let thine ear now be attentive, and thine eyes open, that thou mayest hearken unto the prayer of thy servant, which I pray before thee at this time, day and night, for the children of Israel thy servants, while I confess the sins of the children of Israel, which we have sinned against thee. Yea, I and my father's house have sinned:

NEHEMIAH 1:8-9

Remember, I beseech thee, the word that thou commandedst thy servant Moses, saying, If ye trespass, I will scatter you abroad among the peoples: but if ye return unto me, and keep my commandments and do them, though your outcasts were in the uttermost part of the heavens, yet will I gather them from thence, and will bring them unto the place that I have chosen, to cause my name to dwell there.

NEHEMIAH 2:20

Then answered I them, and said unto them, The God of heaven, he will prosper us; therefore we his servants will arise and build: but ye have no portion, nor right, nor memorial, in Jerusalem.

NEHEMIAH 4:14

And I looked, and rose up, and said unto the nobles, and to the rulers, and to the rest of the people, Be not ye afraid of them: remember the Lord, who is great and terrible, and fight for your brethren, your sons, and your daughters, your wives, and your houses.

NEHEMIAH 8:10

Then he said unto them, Go your way, eat the fat, and drink the sweet, and send portions unto him for whom nothing is prepared; for this day is holy unto our Lord: neither be ye grieved; for the joy of Jehovah is your strength.

NEHEMIAH 9:8

and foundest his heart faithful before thee, and madest a covenant with him to give the land of the Canaanite, the Hittite, the Amorite, and the Perizzite, and the Jebusite, and the Girgashite, to give it unto his seed, and hast performed thy words; for thou art righteous.

ESTHER 4:13-14

Then Mordecai bade them return answer unto Esther, Think not with thyself that thou shalt escape in the king's house, more than all the Jews. For if thou altogether holdest thy peace at this time, then will relief and deliverance arise to the Jews from another place, but thou and thy father's house will perish: and who knoweth whether thou art not come to the kingdom for such a time as this?

ESTHER 8:16

The Jews had light and gladness, and joy and honor.

JOB 1:21

and he said, Naked came I out of my mother's womb, and naked shall I return thither: Jehovah gave, and Jehovah hath taken away; blessed be the name of Jehovah.

JOB 2:10

But he said unto her, Thou speakest as one of the foolish women speaketh. What? shall we receive good at the hand of God, and shall we not receive evil? In all this did not Job sin with his lips.

JOB 5:17

Behold, happy is the man whom God correcteth: Therefore despise not thou the chastening of the Almighty.

JOB 7:17-18

What is man, that thou shouldest magnify him, and that thou shouldest set thy mind upon him, and that thou shouldest visit him every morning, and try him every moment?

JOB 10:12

Thou hast granted me life and lovingkindness; and thy visitation hath preserved my spirit.

JOB 12:13-14

With *God* is wisdom and might; He hath counsel and understanding. Behold, he breaketh down, and it cannot be built again; He shutteth up a man, and there can be no opening.

JOB 14:14

If a man die, shall he live *again*? All the days of my warfare would I wait, till my release should come.

JOB 16:19

Even now, behold, my witness is in heaven, and he that voucheth for me is on high.

JOB 19:25-27

But as for me I know that my Redeemer liveth, and at last he will stand up upon the earth: And after my skin, *even* this *body*, is destroyed, then without my flesh shall I see God; Whom I, even I, shall see, on my side, and mine eyes shall behold, and not as a stranger. My heart is consumed within me.

JOB 23:10

But he knoweth the way that I take; when he hath tried me, I shall come forth as gold.

JOB 28:28

And unto man he said, behold, the fear of the Lord, that is wisdom; and to depart from evil is understanding.

JOB 37:23-24

Touching the Almighty, we cannot find him out: He is excellent in power; and in justice and plenteous righteousness he will not afflict. Men do therefore fear him: He regardeth not any that are wise of heart.

JOB 42:2

I know that thou canst do all things, and that no purpose of thine can be restrained.

PSALM 1:1-3

Blessed is the man that walketh not in the counsel of the wicked, nor standeth in the way of sinners, nor sitteth in the seat of scoffers: but his delight is in the law of Jehovah; and on his law doth he meditate day and night. And he shall be like a tree planted by the streams of water, that bringeth forth its fruit in its season, whose leaf also doth not wither; and whatsoever he doeth shall prosper.

PSALM 2:12

Kiss the son, lest he be angry, and ye perish in the way, for his wrath will soon be kindled. Blessed are all they that take refuge in him.

PSALM 4:3

But know that Jehovah hath set apart for himself him that is godly: Jehovah will hear when I call unto him.

PSALM 5:12

For thou wilt bless the righteous; O Jehovah, thou wilt compass him with favor as with a shield.

PSALM 9:9-10

Jehovah also will be a high tower for the oppressed, a high tower in times of trouble; and they that know thy name will put their trust in thee; for thou, Jehovah, hast not forsaken them that seek thee.

PSALM 11:7

For Jehovah is righteous; he loveth righteousness: The upright shall behold his face.

PSALM 18:30

As for God, his way is perfect: The word of Jehovah is tried; He is a shield unto all them that take refuge in him.

PSALM 25:12

What man is he that feareth Jehovah? Him shall he instruct in the way that he shall choose.

PSALM 32:8

I will instruct thee and teach thee in the way which thou shalt go: I will counsel thee with mine eye upon thee.

PSALM 32:10

Many sorrows shall be to the wicked; but he that trusteth in Jehovah, lovingkindness shall compass him about.

PSALM 34:22

Jehovah redeemeth the soul of his servants; and none of them that take refuge in him shall be condemned.

PSALM 37:4

Delight thyself also in Jehovah; and he will give thee the desires of thy heart.

PSALM 55:22

Cast thy burden upon Jehovah, and he will sustain thee: He will never suffer the righteous to be moved.

PSALM 84:11-12

For Jehovah God is a sun and a shield: Jehovah will give grace and glory; no good thing will he withhold from them that walk uprightly. O Jehovah of hosts, blessed is the man that trusteth in thee.

PSALM 103:11-12

For as the heavens are high above the earth, so great is his lovingkindness toward them that fear him. As far as the east is from the west, so far hath he removed our transgressions from us.

PSALM 121:8

Jehovah will keep thy going out and thy coming in from this time forth and for evermore.

PSALM 145:17-20

Jehovah is righteous in all his ways, and gracious in all his works. Jehovah is nigh unto all them that call upon him, to all that call upon him in truth. He will fulfil the desire of them that fear him; He also will hear their cry and will save them. Jehovah preserveth all them that love him; but all the wicked will he destroy.

PROVERBS 1:7

The fear of Jehovah is the beginning of knowledge; *but* the foolish despise wisdom and instruction.

PROVERBS 2:6-8

For Jehovah giveth wisdom; out of his mouth *cometh* knowledge and understanding: He layeth up sound wisdom for the upright; *He is* a shield to them that walk in integrity; That he may guard the paths of justice, and preserve the way of his saints.

PROVERBS 3:5-6

Trust in Jehovah with all thy heart, and lean not upon thine own understanding: In all thy ways acknowledge him, and he will direct thy paths.

PROVERBS 3:11-12

My son, despise not the chastening of Jehovah; neither be weary of his reproof: For whom Jehovah loveth he reproveth, even as a father the son in whom he delighteth.

PROVERBS 8:17

I love them that love me; and those that seek me diligently shall find me.

PROVERBS 8:35-36

For whoso findeth me findeth life, and shall obtain favor of Jehovah. But he that sinneth against me wrongeth his own soul: all they that hate me love death.

PROVERBS 9:10

The fear of Jehovah is the beginning of wisdom; and the knowledge of the Holy One is understanding.

PROVERBS 14:27

The fear of Jehovah is a fountain of life, that one may depart from the snares of death.

PROVERBS 15:33

The fear of Jehovah is the instruction of wisdom; and before honor *goeth* humility.

PROVERBS 16:3

Commit thy works unto Jehovah, and thy purposes shall be established.

PROVERBS 18:10

The name of Jehovah is a strong tower; the righteous runneth into it, and is safe.

PROVERBS 19:21

There are many devices in a man's heart; but the counsel of Jehovah, that shall stand.

PROVERBS 19:23

The fear of Jehovah *tendeth* to life; and he *that hath it* shall abide satisfied; He shall not be visited with evil.

PROVERBS 21:30

There is no wisdom nor understanding nor counsel against Jehovah.

PROVERBS 22:4

The reward of humility *and* the fear of Jehovah *is* riches, and honor, and life.

ECCLESIASTES 2:24-26

There is nothing better for a man *than* that he should eat and drink, and make his soul enjoy good in his labor. This also I saw, that it is from the hand of God. For who can eat, or who can have enjoyment, more than I? For to the man that pleaseth him *God* giveth wisdom, and knowledge, and joy; but to the sinner he giveth travail, to gather and to heap up, that he may give to him that pleaseth God. This also is vanity and a striving after wind.

ECCLESIASTES 3:11

He hath made everything beautiful in its time: also he hath set eternity in their heart, yet so that man cannot find out the work that God hath done from the beginning even to the end.

ECCLESIASTES 3:14

I know that, whatsoever God doeth, it shall be for ever: nothing can be put to it, nor anything taken from it; and God hath done it, that men should fear before him.

ECCLESIASTES 5:18-19

Behold, that which I have seen to be good and to be comely is for one to eat and to drink, and to enjoy good in all his labor, wherein he laboreth under the sun, all the days of his life which God hath given him: for this is his portion. Every man also to whom God hath given riches and wealth, and hath given him power to eat thereof, and to take his portion, and to rejoice in his labor—this is the gift of God.

ECCLESIASTES 8:12

Though a sinner do evil a hundred times, and prolong his *days*, yet surely I know that it shall be well with them that fear God, that fear before him:

ECCLESIASTES 12:13-14

This is the end of the matter; all hath been heard: Fear God, and keep his commandments; for this is the whole *duty* of man. For God will bring every work into judgment, with every hidden thing, whether it be good, or whether it be evil.

SONG OF SOLOMON 2:4

He brought me to the banqueting-house, and his banner over me was love.

SONG OF SOLOMON 2:16

My beloved is mine, and I am his: He feedeth *his flock* among the lilies.

SONG OF SOLOMON 6:3

I am my beloved's, and my beloved is mine: He feedeth *his flock* among the lilies.

SONG OF SOLOMON 7:10

I am my beloved's; and his desire is toward me.

SONG OF SOLOMON 8:6-7

Set me as a seal upon thy heart, as a seal upon thine arm: For love is strong as death; jealousy is cruel as Sheol; the flashes thereof are flashes of fire, a very flame of Jehovah. Many waters cannot quench love, neither can floods drown it: if a man would give all the substance of his house for love, he would utterly be contemned.

ISAIAH 1:18

Come now, and let us reason together, saith Jehovah: though your sins be as scarlet, they shall be as white as snow; though they be red like crimson, they shall be as wool.

ISAIAH 2:4

And he will judge between the nations, and will decide concerning many peoples; and they shall beat their swords into plowshares, and their spears into pruning-hooks; nation shall not lift up sword against nation, neither shall they learn war any more.

ISAIAH 4:2

In that day shall the branch of Jehovah be beautiful and glorious, and the fruit of the land shall be excellent and comely for them that are escaped of Israel.

ISAIAH 7:14

Therefore the Lord himself will give you a sign: behold, a virgin shall conceive, and bear a son, and shall call his name Immanuel.

ISAIAH 9:6-7

For unto us a child is born, unto us a son is given; and the government shall be upon his shoulder: and his name shall be called Wonderful, Counsellor, Mighty God, Everlasting Father, Prince of Peace. Of the increase of his government and of peace there shall be no end, upon the throne of David, and upon his kingdom, to establish it, and to uphold it with justice and with righteousness from henceforth even for ever. The zeal of Jehovah of hosts will perform this.

ISAIAH 11:1-3

And there shall come forth a shoot out of the stock of Jesse, and a branch out of his roots shall bear fruit. And the Spirit of Jehovah shall rest upon him, the spirit of wisdom and understanding, the spirit of counsel and might, the spirit of knowledge and of the fear of

Jehovah. And his delight shall be in the fear of Jehovah; and he shall not judge after the sight of his eyes, neither decide after the hearing of his ears;

ISAIAH 11:6-9

And the wolf shall dwell with the lamb, and the leopard shall lie down with the kid; and the calf and the young lion and the fatling together; and a little child shall lead them. And the cow and the bear shall feed; their young ones shall lie down together; and the lion shall eat straw like the ox. And the sucking child shall play on the hole of the asp, and the weaned child shall put his hand on the adder's den. They shall not hurt nor destroy in all my holy mountain; for the earth shall be full of the knowledge of Jehovah, as the waters cover the sea.

ISAIAH 12:2

Behold, God is my salvation; I will trust, and will not be afraid: for Jehovah, *even* Jehovah, is my strength and song; and he is become my salvation.

ISAIAH 14:27

For Jehovah of hosts hath purposed, and who shall annul it? and his hand is stretched out, and who shall turn it back?

ISAIAH 26:3

Thou wilt keep *him* in perfect peace, *whose* mind *is* stayed *on thee*; because he trusteth in thee.

ISAIAH 30:15

For thus said the Lord Jehovah, the Holy One of Israel, in returning and rest shall ye be saved; in quietness and in confidence shall be your strength.

ISAIAH 30:18

And therefore will Jehovah wait, that he may be gracious unto you; and therefore will he be exalted, that he may have mercy upon you: for Jehovah is a God of justice; blessed are all they that wait for him.

ISAIAH 40:31

but they that wait for Jehovah shall renew their strength; they shall mount up with wings as eagles; they shall run, and not be weary; they shall walk, and not faint.

ISAIAH 41:10

fear thou not, for I am with thee; be not dismayed, for I am thy God; I will strengthen thee; yea, I will help thee; yea, I will uphold thee with the right hand of my righteousness.

ISAIAH 48:17

Thus saith Jehovah, thy Redeemer, the Holy One of Israel: I am Jehovah thy God, who teacheth thee to profit, who leadeth thee by the way that thou shouldest go.

ISAIAH 53:4-6

Surely he hath borne our griefs, and carried our sorrows; yet we did esteem him stricken, smitten of God, and afflicted. But he was wounded for our transgressions, he was bruised for our iniquities; the chastisement of our peace was upon him; and with his stripes we are healed. All we like sheep have gone astray; we have turned every one to his own way; and Jehovah hath laid on him the iniquity of us all.

ISAIAH 57:15

For thus saith the high and lofty One that inhabiteth eternity, whose name is Holy: I dwell in the high and holy place, with him also that is of a contrite and humble spirit, to revive the spirit of the humble, and to revive the heart of the contrite.

ISAIAH 65:17

For, behold, I create new heavens and a new earth; and the former things shall not be remembered, nor come into mind.

JEREMIAH 1:5

Before I formed thee in the belly I knew thee, and before thou camest forth out of the womb I sanctified thee; I have appointed thee a prophet unto the nations.

JEREMIAH 3:17

At that time they shall call Jerusalem the throne of Jehovah; and all the nations shall be gathered unto it, to the name of Jehovah, to Jerusalem: neither shall they walk any more after the stubbornness of their evil heart.

JEREMIAH 7:5-7

For if ye thoroughly amend your ways and your doings; if ye thoroughly execute justice between a man and his neighbor; if ye oppress not the sojourner, the fatherless, and the widow, and shed not innocent blood in this place, neither walk after other gods to your own hurt: then will I cause you to dwell in this place, in the land that I gave to your fathers, from of old even for evermore.

JEREMIAH 7:23

but this thing I commanded them, saying, Hearken unto my voice, and I will be your God, and ye shall be my people; and walk ye in all the way that I command you, that it may be well with you.

JEREMIAH 9:23-24

Thus saith Jehovah, Let not the wise man glory in his wisdom, neither let the mighty man glory in his might, let not the rich man glory in his riches; but let him that glorieth glory in this, that he hath understanding, and knoweth me, that I am Jehovah who exerciseth lovingkindness, justice, and righteousness, in the earth: for in these things I delight, saith Jehovah.

JEREMIAH 10:23

O Jehovah, I know that the way of man is not in himself; it is not in man that walketh to direct his steps.

JEREMIAH 12:15

And it shall come to pass, after that I have plucked them up, I will return and have compassion on them; and I will bring them again, every man to his heritage, and every man to his land.

JEREMIAH 17:5-7

Thus saith Jehovah: Cursed is the man that trusteth in man, and maketh flesh his arm, and whose heart departeth from Jehovah. For he shall be like the heath in the desert, and shall not see when good cometh, but shall inhabit the parched places in the wilderness, a salt land and not inhabited. Blessed is the man that trusteth in Jehovah, and whose trust Jehovah is.

JEREMIAH 17:10

I, Jehovah, search the mind, I try the heart, even to give every man according to his ways, according to the fruit of his doings.

JEREMIAH 23:5-6

Behold, the days come, saith Jehovah, that I will raise unto David a righteous Branch, and he shall reign as king and deal wisely, and shall execute justice and righteousness in the land. In his days Judah shall be saved, and Israel shall dwell safely; and this is his name whereby he shall be called: Jehovah our righteousness.

JEREMIAH 23:23-24

Am I a God at hand, saith Jehovah, and not a God afar off? Can any hide himself in secret places so that I shall not see him? saith Jehovah. Do not I fill heaven and earth? saith Jehovah.

JEREMIAH 24:6-7

For I will set mine eyes upon them for good, and I will bring them again to this land: and I will build them, and not pull them down; and I will plant them, and not pluck them up. And I will give them a heart to know me, that I am Jehovah: and they shall be my people, and I will be their God; for they shall return unto me with their whole heart.

JEREMIAH 29:11-13

For I know the thoughts that I think toward you, saith Jehovah, thoughts of peace, and not of evil, to give you hope in your latter end. And ye shall call upon me, and ye shall go and pray unto me, and I will hearken unto you. And ye shall seek me, and find me, when ye shall search for me with all your heart.

JEREMIAH 31:33-34

But this is the covenant that I will make with the house of Israel after those days, saith Jehovah: I will put my law in their inward parts, and in their heart will I write it; and I will be their God, and they shall be my people. And they shall teach no more every man his neighbor, and every man his brother, saying, Know Jehovah; for they shall all know me, from the least of them unto the greatest of them, saith Jehovah: for I will forgive their iniquity, and their sin will I remember no more.

JEREMIAH 33:3

Call unto me, and I will answer thee, and will show thee great things, and difficult, which thou knowest not.

LAMENTATIONS 2:17

Jehovah hath done that which he purposed; he hath fulfilled his word that he commanded in the days of old; He hath thrown down, and hath not pitied: and he hath caused the enemy to rejoice over thee; he hath exalted the horn of thine adversaries.

LAMENTATIONS 3:21-23

This I recall to my mind; therefore have I hope. *It is of* Jehovah's lovingkindnesses that we are not consumed, because his compassions fail not. They are new every morning; great is thy faithfulness.

LAMENTATIONS 3:24-26

Jehovah is my portion, saith my soul; therefore will I hope in him. Jehovah is good unto them that wait for him, to the soul that seeketh him. It is good that a man should hope and quietly wait for the salvation of Jehovah.

LAMENTATIONS 3:32-33

For though he cause grief, yet will he have compassion according to the multitude of his lovingkindnesses. For he doth not afflict willingly, nor grieve the children of men.

EZEKIEL 11:19-20

And I will give them one heart, and I will put a new spirit within you; and I will take the stony heart out of their flesh, and will give them a heart of flesh; that they may walk in my statutes, and keep mine ordinances, and do them: and they shall be my people, and I will be their God.

EZEKIEL 18:32

For I have no pleasure in the death of him that dieth, saith the Lord Jehovah: wherefore turn yourselves, and live.

EZEKIEL 20:41-44

As a sweet savor will I accept you, when I bring you out from the peoples, and gather you out of the countries wherein ye have been scattered; and I will be sanctified in you in the sight of the nations. And ye shall know that I am Jehovah, when I shall bring you into the land of Israel, into the country which I sware to give unto your fathers. And there shall ye remember your ways, and all your doings, wherein ye have polluted yourselves; and ye shall loathe yourselves in your own sight for all your evils that ye have committed. And ye shall know that I am Jehovah, when I have dealt with you for my name's sake, not according to your evil ways, nor according to your corrupt doings, O ye house of Israel, saith the Lord Jehovah.

EZEKIEL 33:11

Say unto them, As I live, saith the Lord Jehovah, I have no pleasure in the death of the wicked; but that the wicked turn from his way and live: turn ye, turn ye from your evil ways; for why will ye die, O house of Israel?

EZEKIEL 34:11-16

For thus saith the Lord Jehovah: Behold, I myself, even I, will search for my sheep, and will seek them out. As a shepherd seeketh out his flock in the day that he is among his sheep that are scattered abroad, so will I seek out my sheep; and I will deliver them out of all places whither they have been scattered in the cloudy and dark day. And I will bring them out from the peoples, and gather them from the countries, and will bring them into their own land; and I will feed them upon the mountains of Israel, by the watercourses, and in all the inhabited places of the country. I will feed them with good pasture; and upon the mountains of the height of Israel shall their fold be: there shall they lie down in a good fold; and on fat pasture shall they feed upon the mountains of Israel. I myself will be the shepherd of my sheep, and I will cause them to lie down, saith the Lord Jehovah. I will seek that which was lost, and will bring back that which was driven away, and will bind up that which was broken, and will strengthen that which was sick: but the fat and the strong I will destroy; I will feed them in justice.

EZEKIEL 34:23-24

And I will set up one shepherd over them, and he shall feed them, even my servant David; he shall feed them, and he shall be their shepherd. And I, Jehovah, will be their God, and my servant David prince among them; I, Jehovah, have spoken it.

EZEKIEL 36:26-28

A new heart also will I give you, and a new spirit will I put within you; and I will take away the stony heart out of your flesh, and I will give you a heart of flesh. And I will put my Spirit within you, and cause you to walk in my statutes, and ye shall keep mine ordinances, and do them. And ye shall dwell in the land that I gave to your fathers; and ye shall be my people, and I will be your God.

EZEKIEL 37:13-14

And ye shall know that I am Jehovah, when I have opened your graves, and caused you to come up out of your graves, O my people. And I will put my Spirit in you, and ye shall live, and I will place you in your own land: and ye shall know that I, Jehovah, have spoken it and performed it, saith Jehovah.

EZEKIEL 39:29

neither will I hide my face any more from them; for I have poured out my Spirit upon the house of Israel, saith the Lord Jehovah.

DANIEL 2:20-22

Daniel answered and said, Blessed be the name of God for ever and ever; for wisdom and might are his. And he changeth the times and the seasons; he removeth kings, and setteth up kings; he giveth wisdom unto the wise, and knowledge to them that have understanding; he revealeth the deep and secret things; he knoweth what is in the darkness, and the light dwelleth with him.

DANIEL 2:44

And in the days of those kings shall the God of heaven set up a kingdom which shall never be destroyed, nor shall the sovereignty thereof be left to another people; but it shall break in pieces and consume all these kingdoms, and it shall stand for ever.

DANIEL 4:17

The sentence is by the decree of the watchers, and the demand by the word of the holy ones; to the intent that the living may know that the Most High ruleth in the kingdom of men, and giveth it to whomsoever he will, and setteth up over it the lowest of men.

DANIEL 4:34-35

And at the end of the days I, Nebuchadnezzar, lifted up mine eyes unto heaven, and mine understanding returned unto me, and I blessed the Most High, and I praised and honored him that liveth for ever; for his dominion is an everlasting dominion, and his kingdom from generation to generation; and all the inhabitants of the earth are reputed as nothing; and he doeth according to his will in the army of heaven, and among the inhabitants of the earth; and none can stay his hand, or say unto him, What doest thou?

DANIEL 4:37

Now I, Nebuchadnezzar, praise and extol and honor the King of heaven; for all his works are truth, and his ways justice; and those that walk in pride he is able to abase.

DANIEL 6:26-27

I make a decree, that in all the dominion of my kingdom men tremble and fear before the God of Daniel; for he is the living God, and stedfast for ever, And his kingdom that which shall not be destroyed; and his dominion shall be even unto the end. He delivereth and rescueth, and he worketh signs and wonders in heaven and in earth, who hath delivered Daniel from the power of the lions.

DANIEL 7:14

And there was given him dominion, and glory, and a kingdom, that all the peoples, nations, and languages should serve him: his dominion is an everlasting dominion, which shall not pass away, and his kingdom that which shall not be destroyed.

DANIEL 7:18

But the saints of the Most High shall receive the kingdom, and possess the kingdom for ever, even for ever and ever.

DANIEL 7:27

And the kingdom and the dominion, and the greatness of the kingdoms under the whole heaven, shall be given to the people of the saints of the Most High: his kingdom is an everlasting kingdom, and all dominions shall serve and obey him.

DANIEL 9:4

And I prayed unto Jehovah my God, and made confession, and said, Oh, Lord, the great and dreadful God, who keepeth covenant and lovingkindness with them that love him and keep his commandments.

DANIEL 12:2-3

And many of them that sleep in the dust of the earth shall awake, some to everlasting life, and some to shame and everlasting contempt. And they that are wise shall shine as the brightness of the firmament; and they that turn many to righteousness as the stars for ever and ever.

HOSEA 1:7

But I will have mercy upon the house of Judah, and will save them by Jehovah their God, and will not save them by bow, nor by sword, nor by battle, by horses, nor by horsemen.

HOSEA 1:10-11

Yet the number of the children of Israel shall be as the sand of the sea, which cannot be measured nor numbered; and it shall come to pass that, in the place where it was said unto them, Ye are not my people, it shall be said unto them, *Ye are* the sons of the living God. And the children of Judah and the children of Israel shall be gathered together, and they shall appoint themselves one head, and shall go up from the land; for great shall be the day of Jezreel.

HOSEA 2:19-20

And I will betroth thee unto me for ever; yea, I will betroth thee unto me in righteousness, and in justice, and in lovingkindness, and in mercies. I will even betroth thee unto me in faithfulness; and thou shalt know Jehovah.

HOSEA 2:23

And I will sow her unto me in the earth; and I will have mercy upon her that had not obtained mercy; and I will say to them that were not my people, Thou art my people; and they shall say, *Thou art* my God.

HOSEA 6:6

For I desire goodness, and not sacrifice; and the knowledge of God more than burnt-offerings.

HOSEA 11:4

I drew them with cords of a man, with bands of love; and I was to them as they that lift up the yoke on their jaws; and I laid food before them.

HOSEA 11:9

I will not execute the fierceness of mine anger, I will not return to destroy Ephraim: for I am God, and not man; the Holy One in the midst of thee; and I will not come in wrath.

HOSEA 13:14

I will ransom them from the power of Sheol; I will redeem them from death: O death, where are thy plagues? O Sheol, where is thy destruction? repentance shall be hid from mine eyes.

HOSEA 14:9

Who is wise, that he may understand these things? prudent, that he may know them? for the ways of Jehovah are right, and the just shall walk in them; but transgressors shall fall therein.

JOEL 2:11-13

And Jehovah uttereth his voice before his army; for his camp is very great; for he is strong that executeth his word; for the day of Jehovah is great and very terrible; and who can abide it? Yet even now, saith Jehovah, turn ye unto me with all your heart, and with fasting, and with weeping, and with mourning: and rend your heart, and not your garments, and turn unto Jehovah your God; for he is gracious and merciful, slow to anger, and abundant in lovingkindness, and repenteth him of the evil.

JOEL 2:25-27

And I will restore to you the years that the locust hath eaten, the canker-worm, and the caterpillar, and the palmer-worm, my great army which I sent among you. And ye shall eat in plenty and be satisfied, and shall praise the name of Jehovah your God, that hath dealt wondrously with you; and my people shall never be put to shame. And ye shall know that I am in the midst of Israel, and that I am Jehovah your God, and there is none else; and my people shall never be put to shame.

JOEL 2:28-32

And it shall come to pass afterward, that I will pour out my Spirit upon all flesh; and your sons and your daughters shall prophesy, your old men shall dream dreams, your young men shall see visions: and also upon the servants and upon the handmaids in those days will I pour out my Spirit. And I will show wonders in the heavens and in the earth: blood, and fire, and pillars of smoke. The sun shall be turned into darkness, and the moon into blood, before the great and terrible day of Jehovah cometh. And it shall come to pass, that whosoever shall call on the name of Jehovah shall be delivered; for in mount Zion and in Jerusalem there shall be those that escape, as Jehovah hath said, and among the remnant those whom Jehovah doth call.

JOEL 3:16-18

And Jehovah will roar from Zion, and utter his voice from Jerusalem; and the heavens and the earth shall shake: but Jehovah will be a refuge unto his people, and a stronghold to the children of Israel. o shall ye know that I am Jehovah your God, dwelling in Zion my holy mountain: then shall Jerusalem be holy, and there shall no strangers pass through her any more. And it shall come to pass in that day, that the mountains shall drop down sweet wine, and the hills shall flow with milk, and all the brooks of Judah shall flow with waters; and a fountain shall come forth from the house of Jehovah, and shall water the valley of Shittim.

AMOS 3:7-8

Surely the Lord Jehovah will do nothing, except he reveal his secret unto his servants the prophets. The lion hath roared; who will not fear? The Lord Jehovah hath spoken; who can but prophesy?

AMOS 4:13

For, lo, he that formeth the mountains, and createth the wind, and declareth unto man what is his thought; that maketh the morning darkness, and treadeth upon the high places of the earth—Jehovah, the God of hosts, is his name.

AMOS 5:8

seek him that maketh the Pleiades and Orion, and turneth the shadow of death into the morning, and maketh the day dark with night; that calleth for the waters of the sea, and poureth them out upon the face of the earth (Jehovah is his name);

AMOS 5:21-24

I hate, I despise your feasts, and I will take no delight in your solemn assemblies. Yea, though ye offer me your burnt-offerings and meal-offerings, I will not accept them; neither will I regard the peace-offerings of your fat beasts. Take thou away from me the noise of thy songs; for I will not hear the melody of thy viols. But let justice roll down as waters, and righteousness as a mighty stream.

AMOS 9:13-15

Behold, the days come, saith Jehovah, that the plowman shall overtake the reaper, and the treader of grapes him that soweth seed; and the mountains shall drop sweet wine, and all the hills shall melt. And I will bring back the captivity of my people Israel, and they shall build the waste cities, and inhabit them; and they shall plant vineyards, and drink the wine thereof; they shall also make gardens, and eat the fruit of them. And I will plant them upon their land, and they shall no more be plucked up out of their land which I have given them, saith Jehovah thy God.

OBADIAH 15

For the day of Jehovah is near upon all the nations: as thou hast done, it shall be done unto thee; thy dealing shall return upon thine own head.

OBADIAH 17-18

But in mount Zion there shall be those that escape, and it shall be holy; and the house of Jacob shall possess their possessions. And the house of Jacob shall be a fire, and the house of Joseph a flame, and the house of Esau for stubble, and they shall burn among them, and devour them; and there shall not be any remaining to the house of Esau; for Jehovah hath spoken it.

OBADIAH 21

And saviours shall come up on mount Zion to judge the mount of Esau; and the kingdom shall be Jehovah's.

JONAH 2:2

And he said, I called by reason of mine affliction unto Jehovah, a nd he answered me; Out of the belly of Sheol cried I, *and* thou heardest my voice.

JONAH 2:7-9

When my soul fainted within me, I remembered Jehovah; and my prayer came in unto thee, into thy holy temple. They that regard lying vanities forsake their own mercy. But I will sacrifice unto thee with the voice of thanksgiving; I will pay that which I have vowed. Salvation is of Jehovah.

JONAH 4:2

And he prayed unto Jehovah, and said, I pray thee, O Jehovah, was not this my saying, when I was yet in my country? Therefore I hasted to flee unto Tarshish; for I knew that thou art a gracious God, and merciful, slow to anger, and abundant in lovingkindness, and repentest thee of the evil.

MICAH 2:7

Shall it be said, O house of Jacob, Is the Spirit of Jehovah straitened? are these his doings? Do not my words do good to him that walketh uprightly?

MICAH 4:1-2

But in the latter days it shall come to pass, that the mountain of Jehovah's house shall be established on the top of the mountains, and it shall be exalted above the hills; and peoples shall flow unto it. And many nations shall go and say, Come ye, and let us go up to the mountain of Jehovah, and to the house of the God of Jacob; and he will teach us of his ways, and we will walk in his paths. For out of Zion shall go forth the law, and the word of Jehovah from Jerusalem;

MICAH 4:3

and he will judge between many peoples, and will decide concerning strong nations afar off: and they shall beat their swords into plowshares, and their spears into pruning-hooks; nation shall not lift up sword against nation, neither shall they learn war any more.

MICAH 4:4-5

But they shall sit every man under his vine and under his fig-tree; and none shall make them afraid: for the mouth of Jehovah of hosts hath spoken it. For all the peoples walk every one in the name of his god; and we will walk in the name of Jehovah our God for ever and ever.

MICAH 5:2

But thou, Beth-lehem Ephrathah, which art little to be among the thousands of Judah, out of thee shall one come forth unto me that is to be ruler in Israel; whose goings forth are from of old, from everlasting.

MICAH 6:8

He hath showed thee, O man, what is good; and what doth Jehovah require of thee, but to do justly, and to love kindness, and to walk humbly with thy God?

MICAH 7:7

But as for me, I will look unto Jehovah; I will wait for the God of my salvation: my God will hear me.

MICAH 7:18-19

Who is a God like unto thee, that pardoneth iniquity, and passeth over the transgression of the remnant of his heritage? he retaineth not his anger for ever, because he delighteth in lovingkindness. He will again have compassion upon us; he will tread our iniquities under foot; and thou wilt cast all their sins into the depths of the sea.

NAHUM 1:2-3

Jehovah is a jealous God and avengeth; Jehovah avengeth and is full of wrath; Jehovah taketh vengeance on his adversaries, and he reserveth *wrath* for his enemies. Jehovah is slow to anger, and great in power, and will by no means clear *the guilty*: Jehovah hath his way in the whirlwind and in the storm, and the clouds are the dust of his feet.

NAHUM 1:7

Jehovah is good, a stronghold in the day of trouble; and he knoweth them that take refuge in him.

NAHUM 1:9

What do ye devise against Jehovah? he will make a full end; affliction shall not rise up the second time.

NAHUM 1:12-13

Thus saith Jehovah: Though they be in full strength, and likewise many, even so shall they be cut down, and he shall pass away. Though I have afflicted thee, I will afflict thee no more. And now will I break his yoke from off thee, and will burst thy bonds in sunder.

HABAKKUK 1:13

Thou that art of purer eyes than to behold evil, and that canst not look on perverseness, wherefore lookest thou upon them that deal treacherously, and holdest thy peace when the wicked swalloweth up the man that is more righteous than he;

HABAKKUK 2:4

Behold, his soul is puffed up, it is not upright in him; but the righteous shall live by his faith.

HABAKKUK 2:14

For the earth shall be filled with the knowledge of the glory of Jehovah, as the waters cover the sea.

HABAKKUK 2:20

But Jehovah is in his holy temple: let all the earth keep silence before him.

HABAKKUK 3:2

O Jehovah, I have heard the report of thee, and am afraid: O Jehovah, revive thy work in the midst of the years; in the midst of the years make it known; in wrath remember mercy.

HABAKKUK 3:18-19

Yet I will rejoice in Jehovah, I will joy in the God of my salvation. Jehovah, the Lord, is my strength; and he maketh my feet like hinds' *feet*, and will make me to walk upon my high places.

ZEPHANIAH 1:14-15

The great day of Jehovah is near, it is near and hasteth greatly, *even* the voice of the day of Jehovah; the mighty man crieth there bitterly. That day is a day of wrath, a day of trouble and distress, a day of wasteness and desolation, a day of darkness and gloominess, a day of clouds and thick darkness.

ZEPHANIAH 3:8

Therefore wait ye for me, saith Jehovah, until the day that I rise up to the prey; for my determination is to gather the nations, that I may assemble the kingdoms, to pour upon them mine indignation, even all my fierce anger; for all the earth shall be devoured with the fire of my jealousy.

ZEPHANIAH 3:12

But I will leave in the midst of thee an afflicted and poor people, and they shall take refuge in the name of Jehovah.

ZEPHANIAH 3:17

Jehovah thy God is in the midst of thee, a mighty one who will save; he will rejoice over thee with joy; he will rest in his love; he will joy over thee with singing.

HAGGAI 2:5

according to the word that I covenanted with you when ye came out of Egypt, and my Spirit abode among you: fear ye not.

HAGGAI 2:6-9

For thus saith Jehovah of hosts: Yet once, it is a little while, and I will shake the heavens, and the earth, and the sea, and the dry land; and I will shake all nations; and the precious things of all nations shall come; and I will fill this house with glory, saith Jehovah of hosts. The silver is mine, and the gold is mine, saith Jehovah of hosts. The latter glory of this house shall be greater than the former, saith Jehovah of hosts; and in this place will I give peace, saith Jehovah of hosts.

ZECHARIAH 1:3

Therefore say thou unto them, Thus saith Jehovah of hosts: Return unto me, saith Jehovah of hosts, and I will return unto you, saith Jehovah of hosts.

ZECHARIAH 1:16

Therefore thus saith Jehovah: I am returned to Jerusalem with mercies; my house shall be built in it, saith Jehovah of hosts, and a line shall be stretched forth over Jerusalem.

ZECHARIAH 2:4-5

and said unto him, Run, speak to this young man, saying, Jerusalem shall be inhabited as villages without walls, by reason of the multitude of men and cattle therein. For I, saith Jehovah, will be unto her a wall of fire round about, and I will be the glory in the midst of her.

ZECHARIAH 2:8

For thus saith Jehovah of hosts: After glory hath he sent me unto the nations which plundered you; for he that toucheth you toucheth the apple of his eye.

ZECHARIAH 2:10-13

Sing and rejoice, O daughter of Zion; for, lo, I come, and I will dwell in the midst of thee, saith Jehovah. And many nations shall join themselves to Jehovah in that day, and shall be my people; and I will dwell in the midst of thee, and thou shalt know that Jehovah of hosts hath sent me unto thee. And Jehovah shall inherit Judah as his portion in the holy land, and shall yet choose Jerusalem. Be silent, all flesh, before Jehovah; for he is waked up out of his holy habitation.

ZECHARIAH 4:6

Then he answered and spake unto me, saying, This is the word of Jehovah unto Zerubbabel, saying, Not by might, nor by power, but by my Spirit, saith Jehovah of hosts.

ZECHARIAH 8:3

Thus saith Jehovah: I am returned unto Zion, and will dwell in the midst of Jerusalem: and Jerusalem shall be called The city of truth; and the mountain of Jehovah of hosts, The holy mountain.

ZECHARIAH 8:7

Thus saith Jehovah of hosts: Behold, I will save my people from the east country, and from the west country;

ZECHARIAH 9:9-10

Rejoice greatly, O daughter of Zion; shout, O daughter of Jerusalem: behold, thy king cometh unto thee; he is just, and having salvation; lowly, and riding upon an ass, even upon a colt the foal of an ass. And I will cut off the chariot from Ephraim, and the horse from Jerusalem; and the battle bow shall be cut off; and he shall speak peace unto the nations: and his dominion shall be from sea to sea, and from the River to the ends of the earth.

ZECHARIAH 12:10

And I will pour upon the house of David, and upon the inhabitants of Jerusalem, the spirit of grace and of supplication; and they shall look unto me whom they have pierced; and they shall mourn for him, as one mourneth for his only son, and shall be in bitterness for him, as one that is in bitterness for his first-born.

ZECHARIAH 14:4-5

And his feet shall stand in that day upon the mount of Olives, which is before Jerusalem on the east; and the mount of Olives shall be cleft in the midst thereof toward the east and toward the west, *and there shall be* a very great valley; and half of the mountain shall remove toward the north, and half of it toward the south. And ye shall flee by the valley of my mountains; for the valley of the mountains shall reach unto Azel; yea, ye shall flee, like as ye fled from before the earthquake in the days of Uzziah king of Judah; and

Jehovah my God shall come, and all the holy ones with thee.

ZECHARIAH 14:9

And Jehovah shall be King over all the earth: in that day shall Jehovah be one, and his name one.

MALACHI 1:11

For from the rising of the sun even unto the going down of the same my name *shall be* great among the Gentiles; and in every place incense *shall be* offered unto my name, and a pure offering: for my name *shall be* great among the Gentiles, saith Jehovah of hosts.

MALACHI 3:1-3

Behold, I send my messenger, and he shall prepare the way before me: and the Lord, whom ye seek, will suddenly come to his temple; and the messenger of the covenant, whom ye desire, behold, he cometh, saith Jehovah of hosts. But who can abide the day of his coming? and who shall stand when he appeareth? for he is like a refiner's fire, and like fullers' soap: and he will sit as a refiner and purifier of silver, and he will purify the sons of Levi, and refine them as gold and silver; and they shall offer unto Jehovah offerings in righteousness.

MALACHI 3:6

For I, Jehovah, change not; therefore ye, O sons of Jacob, are not consumed.

MALACHI 3:7

From the days of your fathers ye have turned aside from mine ordinances, and have not kept them. Return unto me, and I will return unto you, saith Jehovah of hosts. But ye say, Wherein shall we return?

MALACHI 4:2

But unto you that fear my name shall the sun of righteousness arise with healing in its wings; and ye shall go forth, and gambol as calves of the stall.

MATTHEW 11:28-30

Come unto me, all ye that labor and are heavy laden, and I will give you rest. Take my yoke upon you, and learn of me; for I am meek and lowly in heart: and ye shall find rest unto your souls. For my yoke is easy, and my burden is light.

MATTHEW 28:18-20

And Jesus came to them and spake unto them, saying, All authority hath been given unto me in heaven and on earth. Go ye therefore, and make disciples of all the nations, baptizing them into the name of the Father and of the Son and of the Holy Spirit: teaching them to observe all things whatsoever I commanded you: and lo, I am with you always, even unto the end of the world.

MARK 14:36

And he said, Abba, Father, all things are possible unto thee; remove this cup from me: howbeit not what I will, but what thou wilt.

MARK 2:8-12

And straightway Jesus, perceiving in his spirit that they so reasoned within themselves, saith unto them, Why reason ye these things in your hearts? Which is easier, to say to the sick of the palsy, Thy sins are forgiven; or to say, Arise, and take up thy bed, and walk? But that ye may know that the Son of man hath authority on earth to forgive sins (he saith to the sick of the palsy), I say unto thee, Arise, take up thy bed, and go unto thy house. And he arose, and straightway took up the bed, and went forth before them all; insomuch that they were all amazed, and glorified God, saying, We never saw it on this fashion.

MARK 8:34-37

And he called unto him the multitude with his disciples, and said unto them, If any man would come after me, let him deny himself, and take up his cross, and follow me. For whosoever would save his life shall lose it; and whosoever shall lose his life for my sake and the gospel's shall save it. For what doth it profit a man, to gain the whole world, and forfeit his life? For what should a man give in exchange for his life?

MARK 10:42-45

And Jesus called them to him, and saith unto them, Ye know that they who are accounted to rule over the Gentiles lord it over them; and their great ones exercise authority over them. But it is not so among you: but whosoever would become great among you, shall be your minister; and whosoever would be first among you, shall be servant of all. For the Son of man also came not to be ministered unto, but to minister, and to give his life a ransom for many.

LUKE 1:32-33

He shall be great, and shall be called the Son of the Most High: and the Lord God shall give unto him the throne of his father David: and he shall reign over the house of Jacob for ever; and of his kingdom there shall be no end.

LUKE 12:22-34

And he said unto his disciples, Therefore I say unto you, Be not anxious for *your* life, what ye shall eat; nor yet for your body, what ye shall put on. For the life is more than the food, and the body than the raiment. Consider the ravens, that they sow not, neither reap; which have no store-chamber nor barn; and God feedeth them: of how much more value are ye than the birds! And which of you by being anxious can add a cubit unto the measure of his life? If then ye are not able to do even that which is least, why are ye anxious concerning the rest? Consider the lilies, how they grow: they toil not, neither do they spin; yet I say unto you, Even Solomon in all his glory was not arrayed like one of these. But if God doth so clothe the grass in the field, which to-day is, and to-morrow is cast into the oven; how much more *shall he clothe* you, O ye of little faith? And seek not ye what ye shall eat, and what ye shall drink, neither be ye of doubtful mind. For all these things do the nations of the world seek after: but your Father knoweth that ye have need of these things. Yet seek ye his kingdom, and these things shall be added unto you. Fear not, little flock; for it is your Father's good pleasure to give you the kingdom. Sell that which ye have, and give alms; make for yourselves purses which wax not old, a treasure in the heavens that faileth not, where no thief draweth near, neither moth destroyeth. For where your treasure is, there will your heart be also.

LUKE 7:47-49

Wherefore I say unto thee, Her sins, which are many, are forgiven; for she loved much: but to whom little is forgiven, *the same* loveth little. And he said unto her, Thy sins are forgiven. And they that sat at meat with him began to say within themselves, Who is this that even forgiveth sins?

LUKE 10:20

Nevertheless in this rejoice not, that the spirits are subject unto you; but rejoice that your names are written in heaven.

JOHN 1:12

But as many as received him, to them gave he the right to become children of God, *even* to them that believe on his name:

JOHN 3:16

For God so loved the world, that he gave his only begotten Son, that whosoever believeth on him should not perish, but have eternal life.

JOHN 5:24

Verily, verily, I say unto you, He that heareth my word, and believeth him that sent me, hath eternal life, and cometh not into judgment, but hath passed out of death into life.

JOHN 10:9-10

I am the door; by me if any man enter in, he shall be saved, and shall go in and go out, and shall find pasture. The thief cometh not, but that he may steal, and kill, and destroy: I came that they may have life, and may have *it* abundantly.

JOHN 11:25-26

Jesus said unto her, I am the resurrection, and the life: he that believeth on me, though he die, yet shall he live; and whosoever liveth and believeth on me shall never die. Believest thou this?

JOHN 15:1-8

I am the true vine, and my Father is the husbandman. Every branch in me that beareth not fruit, he taketh it away: and every *branch* that beareth fruit, he cleanseth it, that it may bear more fruit. Already ye are clean because of the word which I have spoken unto you. Abide in me, and I in you. As the branch cannot bear fruit of itself, except it abide in the vine; so neither can ye, except ye abide in me. I am the vine, ye are the branches: He that abideth in me, and I in him, the same beareth much fruit: for apart from me ye can do nothing. If a man abide not in me, he is cast forth as a branch, and is withered; and they gather them, and cast them into the fire, and they are burned. If ye abide in me, and my words abide in you, ask whatsoever ye will, and it shall be done unto you. Herein is my Father glorified, that ye bear much fruit; and *so* shall ye be my disciples.

JOHN 20:30-31

Many other signs therefore did Jesus in the presence of the disciples, which are not written in this book: but these are written, that ye may believe that Jesus is the Christ, the Son of God; and that believing ye may have life in his name.

ACTS 1:8

But ye shall receive power, when the Holy Spirit is come upon you: and ye shall be my witnesses both in Jerusalem, and in all Judaea and Samaria, and unto the uttermost part of the earth.

ACTS 10:40-43

Him God raised up the third day, and gave him to be made manifest, not to all the people, but unto witnesses that were chosen before of God, *even* to us, who ate and drank with him after he rose from the dead. And he charged us to preach unto the people, and to testify that this is he who is ordained of God *to be* the Judge of the living and the dead. To him bear all the prophets witness, that through his name every one that believeth on him shall receive remission of sins.

ACTS 4:12

And in none other is there salvation: for neither is there any other name under heaven, that is given among men, wherein we must be saved.

ACTS 4:33

And with great power gave the apostles their witness of the resurrection of the Lord Jesus: and great grace was upon them all.

ACTS 13:32-39

And we bring you good tidings of the promise made unto the fathers, that God hath fulfilled the same unto our children, in that he raised up Jesus; as also it is written in the second psalm, Thou art my Son, this day have I begotten thee. And as concerning that he raised him up from the dead, now no more to return to corruption, he hath spoken on this wise, I will give you the holy and sure *blessings* of David. Because he saith also in another *psalm*, Thou wilt not give thy Holy One to see corruption. For David, after he had in his own generation served the counsel of God, fell asleep, and was laid unto his fathers, and saw corruption: but he whom God raised up saw no corruption. Be it known unto you therefore, brethren, that through this man is proclaimed unto you remission of sins: and by him every one that believeth is justified from all things, from which ye could not be justified by the law of Moses.

ACTS 17:27-28

that they should seek God, if haply they might feel after him and find him, though he is not far from each one of us: for in him we live, and move, and have our being; as certain even of your own poets have said, For we are also his offspring.

ROMANS 1:16-17

For I am not ashamed of the gospel: for it is the power of God unto salvation to every one that believeth; to the Jew first, and also to the Greek. For therein is revealed a righteousness of God from faith unto faith: as it is written, But the righteous shall live by faith.

ROMANS 3:23-25

for all have sinned, and fall short of the glory of God; being justified freely by his grace through the redemption that is in Christ Jesus: whom God set forth *to be* a propitiation, through faith, in his blood, to show his righteousness because of the passing over of the sins done aforetime, in the forbearance of God;

ROMANS 6:5-11

For if we have become united with *him* in the likeness of his death, we shall be also *in the likeness* of his resurrection; knowing this, that our old man was crucified with *him*, that the body of sin might be done away, that so we should no longer be in bondage to sin; for he that hath died is justified from sin. But if we died with Christ, we believe that we shall also live with him; knowing that Christ being raised from the dead dieth no more; death no more hath dominion over him. For the death that he died, he died unto sin once: but the life that he liveth, he liveth unto God. Even so reckon ye also yourselves to be dead unto sin, but alive unto God in Christ Jesus.

ROMANS 8:18

For I reckon that the sufferings of this present time are not worthy to be compared with the glory which shall be revealed to us-ward.

ROMANS 8:28-29

And we know that to them that love God all things work together for good, *even* to them that are called according to *his* purpose. For whom he foreknew, he also foreordained *to be* conformed to the image of his Son, that he might be the firstborn among many brethren:

ROMANS 12:2

And be not fashioned according to this world: but be ye transformed by the renewing of your mind, that ye may prove what is the good and acceptable and perfect will of God.

I CORINTHIANS 1:2

unto the church of God which is at Corinth, *even* them that are sanctified in Christ Jesus, called *to be* saints, with all that call upon the name of our Lord Jesus Christ in every place, their *Lord* and ours:

I CORINTHIANS 1:18

For the word of the cross is to them that perish foolishness; but unto us who are saved it is the power of God.

I CORINTHIANS 2:9

but as it is written, Things which eye saw not, and ear heard not, and *which* entered not into the heart of man, whatsoever things God prepared for them that love him.

I CORINTHIANS 3:22-23

whether Paul, or Apollos, or Cephas, or the world, or life, or death, or things present, or things to come; all are yours; and ye are Christ's; and Christ is God's.

I CORINTHIANS 6:19-20

Or know ye not that your body is a temple of the Holy Spirit which is in you, which ye have from God? and ye are not your own; for ye were bought with a price: glorify God therefore in your body.

I CORINTHIANS 15:22

For as in Adam all die, so also in Christ shall all be made alive.

I CORINTHIANS 15:58

Wherefore, my beloved brethren, be ye stedfast, unmoveable, always abounding in the work of the Lord, forasmuch as ye know that your labor is not vain in the Lord.

2 CORINTHIANS 1:3-4

Blessed *be* the God and Father of our Lord Jesus Christ, the Father of mercies and God of all comfort; who comforteth us in all our affliction, that we may be able to comfort them that are in any affliction, through the comfort wherewith we ourselves are comforted of God.

2 CORINTHIANS 2:14

But thanks be unto God, who always leadeth us in triumph in Christ, and maketh manifest through us the savor of his knowledge in every place.

2 CORINTHIANS 3:18

But we all, with unveiled face beholding as in a mirror the glory of the Lord, are transformed into the same image from glory to glory, even as from the Lord the Spirit.

2 CORINTHIANS 4:7

But we have this treasure in earthen vessels, that the exceeding greatness of the power may be of God, and not from ourselves;

2 CORINTHIANS 5:17

Wherefore if any man is in Christ, *he is* a new creature: the old things are passed away; behold, they are become new.

2 CORINTHIANS 5:21

Him who knew no sin he made *to be* sin on our behalf; that we might become the righteousness of God in him.

2 CORINTHIANS 9:6-8

But this *I say*, He that soweth sparingly shall reap also sparingly; and he that soweth bountifully shall reap also bountifully. *Let* each man *do* according as he hath purposed in his heart: not grudgingly, or of necessity: for God loveth a cheerful giver. And God is able to make all grace abound unto you; that ye, having always all sufficiency in everything, may abound unto every good work:

GALATIANS 1:3-4

Grace to you and peace from God the Father, and our Lord Jesus Christ, who gave himself for our sins, that he might deliver us out of this present evil world, according to the will of our God and Father:

GALATIANS 2:20

I have been crucified with Christ; and it is no longer I that live, but Christ liveth in me: and that *life* which I now live in the flesh I live in faith, *the faith* which is in the Son of God, who loved me, and gave himself up for me.

GALATIANS 3:13

Christ redeemed us from the curse of the law, having become a curse for us; for it is written, Cursed is every one that hangeth on a tree:

GALATIANS 3:27-29

For as many of you as were baptized into Christ did put on Christ. There can be neither Jew nor Greek, there can be neither bond nor free, there can be no male and female; for ye all are one *man* in Christ Jesus. And if ye are Christ's, then are ye Abraham's seed, heirs according to promise.

GALATIANS 5:16

But I say, Walk by the Spirit, and ye shall not fulfil the lust of the flesh.

GALATIANS 5:25

If we live by the Spirit, by the Spirit let us also walk.

GALATIANS 5:22-23

But the fruit of the Spirit is love, joy, peace, longsuffering, kindness, goodness, faithfulness, meekness, self-control; against such there is no law.

EPHESIANS 1:3

Blessed *be* the God and Father of our Lord Jesus Christ, who hath blessed us with every spiritual blessing in the heavenly *places* in Christ:

EPHESIANS 1:4

even as he chose us in him before the foundation of the world, that we should be holy and without blemish before him in love:

EPHESIANS 2:8

for by grace have ye been saved through faith; and that not of yourselves, *it is* the gift of God;

EPHESIANS 2:10

For we are his workmanship, created in Christ Jesus for good works, which God afore prepared that we should walk in them.

EPHESIANS 3:20

Now unto him that is able to do exceeding abundantly above all that we ask or think, according to the power that worketh in us,

EPHESIANS 4:24

and put on the new man, that after God hath been created in righteousness and holiness of truth.

EPHESIANS 5:8

for ye were once darkness, but are now light in the Lord: walk as children of light

PHILIPPIANS 1:6

being confident of this very thing, that he who began a good work in you will perfect it until the day of Jesus Christ:

PHILIPPIANS 1:9-11

And this I pray, that your love may abound yet more and more in knowledge and all discernment; so that ye may approve the things that are excellent; that ye may be sincere and void of offence unto the day of Christ; being filled with the fruits of righteousness, which are through Jesus Christ, unto the glory and praise of God.

PHILIPPIANS 1:21

For to me to live is Christ, and to die is gain.

PHILIPPIANS 2:10-11

that in the name of Jesus every knee should bow, of *things* in heaven and *things* on earth and *things* under the earth, and that every tongue should confess that Jesus Christ is Lord, to the glory of God the Father.

PHILIPPIANS 2:13

for it is God who worketh in you both to will and to work, for his good pleasure.

PHILIPPIANS 4:6-7

In nothing be anxious; but in everything by prayer and supplication with thanksgiving let your requests be made known unto God. And the peace of God, which passeth all understanding, shall guard your hearts and your thoughts in Christ Jesus.

PHILIPPIANS 4:19

And my God shall supply every need of yours according to his riches in glory in Christ Jesus.

COLOSSIANS 1:12

giving thanks unto the Father, who made us meet to be partakers of the inheritance of the saints in light.

COLOSSIANS 1:13

who delivered us out of the power of darkness, and translated us into the kingdom of the Son of his love.

COLOSSIANS 1:22

yet now hath he reconciled in the body of his flesh through death, to present you holy and without blemish and unreproveable before him:

COLOSSIANS 1:27

to whom God was pleased to make known what is the riches of the glory of this mystery among the Gentiles, which is Christ in you, the hope of glory:

COLOSSIANS 2:10

and in him ye are made full, who is the head of all principality and power:

COLOSSIANS 2:13

And you, being dead through your trespasses and the uncircumcision of your flesh, you, *I say,* did he make alive together with him, having forgiven us all our trespasses;

COLOSSIANS 3:1-4

If then ye were raised together with Christ, seek the things that are above, where Christ is, seated on the right hand of God. Set your mind on the things that are above, not on the things that are upon the earth. For ye died, and your life is hid with Christ in God. When Christ, *who is* our life, shall be manifested, then shall ye also with him be manifested in glory.

COLOSSIANS 3:12

Put on therefore, as God's elect, holy and beloved, a heart of compassion, kindness, lowliness, meekness, longsuffering;

I THESSALONIANS 1:10

and to wait for his Son from heaven, whom he raised from the dead, *even* Jesus, who delivereth us from the wrath to come.

I THESSALONIANS 2:19-20

For what is our hope, or joy, or crown of glorying? Are not even ye, before our Lord Jesus at his coming? For ye are our glory and our joy.

I THESSALONIANS 3:13

to the end he may establish your hearts unblamable in holiness before our God and Father, at the coming of our Lord Jesus with all his saints.

I THESSALONIANS 4:16-17

For the Lord himself shall descend from heaven, with a shout, with the voice of the archangel, and with the trump of God: and the dead in Christ shall rise first; then we that are alive, that are left, shall together with them be caught up in the clouds, to meet the Lord in the air: and so shall we ever be with the Lord.

I THESSALONIANS 5:9-10

For God appointed us not unto wrath, but unto the obtaining of salvation through our Lord Jesus Christ, who died for us, that, whether we wake or sleep, we should live together with him.

I THESSALONIANS 5:23

And the God of peace himself sanctify you wholly; and may your spirit and soul and body be preserved entire, without blame at the coming of our Lord Jesus Christ.

2 THESSALONIANS 1:5-10

which is a manifest token of the righteous judgment of God; to the end that ye may be counted worthy of the kingdom of God, for which ye also suffer: if so be that it is a righteous thing with God to recompense affliction to them that afflict you, and to you that are afflicted rest with us, at the revelation of the Lord Jesus from heaven with the angels of his power in flaming fire, rendering vengeance to them that know not God, and to them that obey not the gospel of our Lord Jesus: who shall suffer punishment, *even* eternal destruction from the face of the Lord and from the glory of his might, when he shall come to be glorified in his saints, and to be marvelled at in all them that believed (because our testimony unto you was believed) in that day.

2 THESSALONIANS 1:11-12

To which end we also pray always for you, that our God may count you worthy of your calling, and fulfil every desire of goodness and *every* work of faith, with power; that the name of our Lord Jesus may be glorified in you, and ye in him, according to the grace of our God and the Lord Jesus Christ.

2 THESSALONIANS 2:13-14

But we are bound to give thanks to God always for you, brethren beloved of the Lord, for that God chose you from the beginning unto salvation in sanctification of the Spirit and belief of the truth: whereunto he called you through our gospel, to the obtaining of the glory of our Lord Jesus Christ.

2 THESSALONIANS 3:5

And the Lord direct your hearts into the love of God, and into the patience of Christ.

I TIMOTHY 1:5

But the end of the charge is love out of a pure heart and a good conscience and faith unfeigned:

I TIMOTHY 1:14

and the grace of our Lord abounded exceedingly with faith and love which is in Christ Jesus.

I TIMOTHY 1:15-16

Faithful is the saying, and worthy of all acceptation, that Christ Jesus came into the world to save sinners; of whom I am chief: howbeit for this cause I obtained mercy, that in me as chief might Jesus Christ show forth all his longsuffering, for an ensample of them that should thereafter believe on him unto eternal life.

I TIMOTHY 1:17

Now unto the King eternal, immortal, invisible, the only God, *be* honor and glory for ever and ever. Amen.

I TIMOTHY 2:4

who would have all men to be saved, and come to the knowledge of the truth.

I TIMOTHY 2:5

For there is one God, one mediator also between God and men, *himself* man, Christ Jesus,

I TIMOTHY 4:8

for bodily exercise is profitable for a little; but godliness is profitable for all things, having promise of the life which now is, and of that which is to come.

I TIMOTHY 6:6

But godliness with contentment is great gain:

1 TIMOTHY 6:17

Charge them that are rich in this present world, that they be not highminded, nor have their hope set on the uncertainty of riches, but on God, who giveth us richly all things to enjoy;

2 TIMOTHY 1:7

For God gave us not a spirit of fearfulness; but of power and love and discipline.

2 TIMOTHY 1:9

who saved us, and called us with a holy calling, not according to our works, but according to his own purpose and grace, which was given us in Christ Jesus before times eternal,

2 TIMOTHY 1:10

but hath now been manifested by the appearing of our Saviour Christ Jesus, who abolished death, and brought life and immortality to light through the gospel,

2 TIMOTHY 1:12

For which cause I suffer also these things: yet I am not ashamed; for I know him whom I have believed, and I am persuaded that he is able to guard that which I have committed unto him against that day.

2 TIMOTHY 2:11-13

Faithful is the saying: For if we died with him, we shall also live with him: if we endure, we shall also reign with him: if we shall deny him, he also will deny us: if we are faithless, he abideth faithful; for he cannot deny himself.

2 TIMOTHY 4:8

henceforth there is laid up for me the crown of righteousness, which the Lord, the righteous judge, shall give to me at that day; and not to me only, but also to all them that have loved his appearing.

2 TIMOTHY 4:18

The Lord will deliver me from every evil work, and will save me unto his heavenly kingdom: to whom *be* the glory for ever and ever. Amen.

TITUS 1:1-2

Paul, a servant of God, and an apostle of Jesus Christ, according to the faith of God's elect, and the knowledge of the truth which is according to godliness, in hope of eternal life, which God, who cannot lie, promised before times eternal;

TITUS 2:11

For the grace of God hath appeared, bringing salvation to all men.

TITUS 2:13-14

looking for the blessed hope and appearing of the glory of the great God and our Saviour Jesus Christ; who gave himself for us, that he might redeem us from all iniquity, and purify unto himself a people for his own possession, zealous of good works.

TITUS 3:4-7

But when the kindness of God our Saviour, and his love toward man, appeared, not by works *done* in righteousness, which we did ourselves, but according to his mercy he saved us, through the washing of regeneration and renewing of the Holy Spirit, which he poured out upon us richly, through Jesus Christ our Saviour; that, being justified by his grace, we might be made heirs according to the hope of eternal life.

PHILEMON 3

Grace to you and peace from God our Father and the Lord Jesus Christ.

PHILEMON 6

that the fellowship of thy faith may become effectual, in the knowledge of every good thing which is in you, unto Christ.

PHILEMON 25

The grace of our Lord Jesus Christ be with your spirit. Amen.

HEBREWS 2:9

But we behold him who hath been made a little lower than the angels, *even* Jesus, because of the suffering of death crowned with glory and honor, that by the grace of God he should taste of death for every *man*.

HEBREWS 2:18

For in that he himself hath suffered being tempted, he is able to succor them that are tempted.

HEBREWS 4:15

For we have not a high priest that cannot be touched with the feeling of our infirmities; but one that hath been in all points tempted like as *we are, yet* without sin.

HEBREWS 4:16

Let us therefore draw near with boldness unto the throne of grace, that we may receive mercy, and may find grace to help *us* in time of need.

HEBREWS 6:19

which we have as an anchor of the soul, *a hope* both sure and stedfast and entering into that which is within the veil;

HEBREWS 7:25

Wherefore also he is able to save to the uttermost them that draw near unto God through him, seeing he ever liveth to make intercession for them.

HEBREWS 9:15

And for this cause he is the mediator of a new covenant, that a death having taken place for the redemption of the transgressions that were under the first covenant, they that have been called may receive the promise of the eternal inheritance.

HEBREWS 11:1

Now faith is assurance of *things* hoped for, a conviction of things not seen.

HEBREWS 11:6

and without faith it is impossible to be well-pleasing *unto him*; for he that cometh to God must believe that he is, and *that* he is a rewarder of them that seek after him.

HEBREWS 13:8

Jesus Christ *is* the same yesterday and to-day, *yea* and for ever.

JAMES 1:17

Every good gift and every perfect gift is from above, coming down from the Father of lights, with whom can be no variation, neither shadow that is cast by turning.

JAMES 1:25

But he that looketh into the perfect law, the *law* of liberty, and *so* continueth, being not a hearer that forgetteth but a doer that worketh, this man shall be blessed in his doing.

JAMES 2:13

For judgment *is* without mercy to him that hath showed no mercy: mercy glorieth against judgment.

JAMES 3:17

But the wisdom that is from above is first pure, then peaceable, gentle, easy to be entreated, full of mercy and good fruits, without variance, without hypocrisy.

JAMES 4:7

Be subject therefore unto God; but resist the devil, and he will flee from you.

JAMES 4:8

Draw nigh to God, and he will draw nigh to you. Cleanse your hands, ye sinners; and purify your hearts, ye doubleminded.

JAMES 5:20

let him know, that he who converteth a sinner from the error of his way shall save a soul from death, and shall cover a multitude of sins.

I PETER 1:2

according to the foreknowledge of God the Father, in sanctification of the Spirit, unto obedience and sprinkling of the blood of Jesus Christ: Grace to you and peace be multiplied.

I PETER 1:3-4

Blessed *be* the God and Father of our Lord Jesus Christ, who according to his great mercy begat us again unto a living hope by the resurrection of Jesus Christ from the dead, unto an inheritance incorruptible, and undefiled, and that fadeth not away, reserved in heaven for you,

I PETER 1:18-19

knowing that ye were redeemed, not with corruptible things, with silver or gold, from your vain manner of life handed down from your fathers; but with precious blood, as of a lamb without blemish and without spot, *even the blood* of Christ:

I PETER 1:23

having been begotten again, not of corruptible seed, but of incorruptible, through the word of God, which liveth and abideth.

I PETER 2:9

But ye are an elect race, a royal priesthood, a holy nation, a people for *God's* own possession, that ye may show forth the excellencies of him who called you out of darkness into his marvellous light:

I PETER 2:24

who his own self bare our sins in his body upon the tree, that we, having died unto sins, might live unto righteousness; by whose stripes ye were healed.

I PETER 3:18

Because Christ also suffered for sins once, the righteous for the unrighteous, that he might bring us to God; being put to death in the flesh, but made alive in the spirit;

I PETER 5:7

casting all your anxiety upon him, because he careth for you.

I PETER 5:10

And the God of all grace, who called you unto his eternal glory in Christ, after that ye have suffered a little while, shall himself perfect, establish, strengthen you.

2 PETER 1:3

seeing that his divine power hath granted unto us all things that pertain unto life and godliness, through the knowledge of him that called us by his own glory and virtue;

2 PETER 1:4

whereby he hath granted unto us his precious and exceeding great promises; that through these ye may become partakers of the divine nature, having escaped from the corruption that is in the world by lust.

2 PETER 1:5-11

Yea, and for this very cause adding on your part all diligence, in your faith supply virtue; and in *your* virtue knowledge; and in *your* knowledge self-control; and in *your* self-control patience; and in *your* patience godliness; and in *your* godliness brotherly kindness; and in *your* brotherly kindness love. For if these things are yours and abound, they make you to be not idle nor unfruitful unto the knowledge of our Lord Jesus Christ. For he that lacketh these things is blind, seeing only what is near, having forgotten the cleansing from his old sins. Wherefore, brethren, give the more diligence to make your calling and election sure: for if ye do these things, ye shall never stumble: for thus shall be richly supplied unto you the entrance into the eternal kingdom of our Lord and Saviour Jesus Christ.

2 PETER 3:8-9

But forget not this one thing, beloved, that one day is with the Lord as a thousand years, and a thousand years as one day. The Lord is not slack concerning his promise, as some count slackness; but is longsuffering to you-ward, not wishing that any should perish, but that all should come to repentance.

2 PETER 3:13

But, according to his promise, we look for new heavens and a new earth, wherein dwelleth righteousness.

I JOHN 1:5

And this is the message which we have heard from him and announce unto you, that God is light, and in him is no darkness at all.

I JOHN 1:7

but if we walk in the light, as he is in the light, we have fellowship one with another, and the blood of Jesus his Son cleanseth us from all sin.

I JOHN 1:9

If we confess our sins, he is faithful and righteous to forgive us our sins, and to cleanse us from all unrighteousness.

I JOHN 2:1-2

My little children, these things write I unto you that ye may not sin. And if any man sin, we have an Advocate with the Father, Jesus Christ the righteous: and he is the propitiation for our sins; and not for ours only, but also for the whole world.

I JOHN 2:17

And the world passeth away, and the lust thereof: but he that doeth the will of God abideth for ever.

I JOHN 3:1

Behold what manner of love the Father hath bestowed upon us, that we should be called children of God; and *such* we are. For this cause the world knoweth us not, because it knew him not.

I JOHN 3:2

Beloved, now are we children of God, and it is not yet made manifest what we shall be. We know that, if he shall be manifested, we shall be like him; for we shall see him even as he is.

I JOHN 4:9-10

Herein was the love of God manifested in us, that God hath sent his only begotten Son into the world that we might live through him. Herein is love, not that we loved God, but that he loved us, and sent his Son *to be* the propitiation for our sins.

I JOHN 4:18

There is no fear in love: but perfect love casteth out fear, because fear hath punishment; and he that feareth is not made perfect in love.

I JOHN 5:1

Whosoever believeth that Jesus is the Christ is begotten of God: and whosoever loveth him that begat loveth him also that is begotten of him.

I JOHN 5:11-12

And the witness is this, that God gave unto us eternal life, and this life is in his Son. He that hath the Son hath the life; he that hath not the Son of God hath not the life.

1 JOHN 5:14-15

And this is the boldness which we have toward him, that, if we ask anything according to his will, he heareth us: and if we know that he heareth us whatsoever we ask, we know that we have the petitions which we have asked of him.

2 JOHN 2

for the truth's sake which abideth in us, and it shall be with us for ever:

2 JOHN 3

Grace, mercy, peace shall be with us, from God the Father, and from Jesus Christ, the Son of the Father, in truth and love.

2 JOHN 6

And this is love, that we should walk after his commandments. This is the commandment, even as ye heard from the beginning, that ye should walk in it.

2 JOHN 9

Whosoever goeth onward and abideth not in the teaching of Christ, hath not God: he that abideth in the teaching, the same hath both the Father and the Son.

3 JOHN 3-4

For I rejoiced greatly, when brethren came and bare witness unto thy truth, even as thou walkest in truth. Greater joy have I none than this, to hear of my children walking in the truth.

3 JOHN 5-8

Beloved, thou doest a faithful work in whatsoever thou doest toward them that are brethren and strangers withal; who bare witness to thy love before the church: whom thou wilt do well to set forward on their journey worthily of God: because that for the sake of the Name they went forth, taking nothing of the Gentiles. We therefore ought to welcome such, that we may be fellow-workers for the truth.

JUDE 2

Mercy unto you and peace and love be multiplied.

JUDE 20-21

But ye, beloved, building up yourselves on your most holy faith, praying in the Holy Spirit, keep yourselves in the love of God, looking for the mercy of our Lord Jesus Christ unto eternal life.

JUDE 24-25

Now unto him that is able to guard you from stumbling, and to set you before the presence of his glory without blemish in exceeding joy, to the only God our Saviour, through Jesus Christ our Lord, *be* glory, majesty, dominion and power, before all time, and now, and for evermore. Amen.

REVELATION 1:3

Blessed is he that readeth, and they that hear the words of the prophecy, and keep the things that are written therein: for the time is at hand.

REVELATION 1:5-6

and from Jesus Christ, *who is* the faithful witness, the firstborn of the dead, and the ruler of the kings of the earth. Unto him that loveth us, and loosed us from our sins by his blood; and he made us *to be* a kingdom, *to be* priests unto his God and Father; to him *be* the glory and the dominion for ever and ever. Amen.

REVELATION 1:18

and the Living one; and I was dead, and behold, I am alive for evermore, and I have the keys of death and of Hades.

REVELATION 2:7

He that hath an ear, let him hear what the Spirit saith to the churches. To him that overcometh, to him will I give to eat of the tree of life, which is in the Paradise of God.

REVELATION 2:11

He that hath an ear, let him hear what the Spirit saith to the churches. He that overcometh shall not be hurt of the second death.

REVELATION 2:17

He that hath an ear, let him hear what the Spirit saith to the churches. To him that overcometh, to him will I give of the hidden manna, and I will give him a white stone, and upon the stone a new name written, which no one knoweth but he that receiveth it.

REVELATION 2:26-27

And he that overcometh, and he that keepeth my works unto the end, to him will I give authority over the nations: and he shall rule them with a rod of iron, as the vessels of the potter are broken to shivers; as I also have received of my Father:

REVELATION 3:5-6

He that overcometh shall thus be arrayed in white garments; and I will in no wise blot his name out of the book of life, and I will confess his name before my Father, and before his angels. He that hath an ear, let him hear what the Spirit saith to the churches.

REVELATION 3:12-13

He that overcometh, I will make him a pillar in the temple of my God, and he shall go out thence no more: and I will write upon him the name of my God, and the name of the city of my God, the new Jerusalem, which cometh down out of heaven from my God, and mine own new name. He that hath an ear, let him hear what the Spirit saith to the churches.

REVELATION 3:20-22

Behold, I stand at the door and knock: if any man hear my voice and open the door, I will come in to him, and will sup with him, and he with me. He that overcometh, I will give to him to sit down with me in my throne, as I also overcame, and sat down with my Father in his throne. He that hath an ear, let him hear what the Spirit saith to the churches.

REVELATION 5:9

And they sing a new song, saying, worthy art thou to take the book, and to open the seals thereof: for thou wast slain, and didst purchase unto God with thy blood *men* of every tribe, and tongue, and people, and nation.

REVELATION 11:15

And the seventh angel sounded; and there followed great voices in heaven, and they said, The kingdom of the world is become *the kingdom* of our Lord, and of his Christ: and he shall reign for ever and ever.

REVELATION 20:6

Blessed and holy is he that hath part in the first resurrection: over these the second death hath no power; but they shall be priests of God and of Christ, and shall reign with him a thousand years.

REVELATION 21:4

and he shall wipe away every tear from their eyes; and death shall be no more; neither shall there be mourning, nor crying, nor pain, any more: the first things are passed away.

REVELATION 21:6-7

And he said unto me, They are come to pass. I am the Alpha and the Omega, the beginning and the end. I will give unto him that is athirst of the fountain of the water of life freely. He that overcometh shall inherit these things; and I will be his God, and he shall be my son.

REVELATION 22:17

And the Spirit and the bride say, Come. And he that heareth, let him say, Come. And he that is athirst, let him come: he that will, let him take the water of life freely.

www.ingramcontent.com/pod-product-compliance
Lightning Source LLC
LaVergne TN
LVHW010947110826
845149LV00015B/3247

* 9 7 8 1 9 5 8 4 0 4 6 9 0 *